Discern

LISTENING FOR
GOD'S WHISPERS

Discern

LISTENING FOR
GOD'S WHISPERS

MARK E. THIBODEAUX, SJ

LOYOLAPRESS.
A JESUIT MINISTRY

LOYOLA PRESS.
A JESUIT MINISTRY

www.loyolapress.com

ISBN-13: 978-0-8294-5991-3
Library of Congress Control Number: 2024943662

Published in Chicago, IL
Printed in the United States of America.
24 25 26 27 28 29 30 31 31 32 Versa 10 9 8 7 6 5 4 3 2 1

And he said, "Go out and stand on the mount before the LORD." And behold, the LORD passed by, and a great and strong wind tore the mountains and broke in pieces the rocks before the LORD, but the LORD was not in the wind. And after the wind an earthquake, but the LORD was not in the earthquake. And after the earthquake a fire, but the LORD was not in the fire. And after the fire the sound of a low whisper. And when Elijah heard it, he wrapped his face in his cloak and went out and stood at the entrance of the cave. And behold, there came a voice to him and said, "What are you doing here, Elijah?"
1 Kings 19:11-13

A Note to Readers

Aren't even our ordinary days sometimes chock-full of tasks and challenges that feel like our very own driving winds, splitting rocks, earthquakes and fires? No wonder we long to hear God in the "still small" voice that quiets us down and centers us again in the peaceful hurricane's eye that we call the soul. And God desires that for us, too. Though often hard to perceive in the midst of the everyday equivalent of storms and earthquakes, the quiet voice of our Creator is never fully snuffed out. It is always there, always whispering God's love for us.

Though we sometimes might wish that God spoke a little more loudly to us, that's often not God's way. The voice of God is usually subtle and gentle, which can lead to some difficulties when everything around us is seemingly so boisterous. This book was created to help you perceive that quiet voice of God in the midst of your noisy life. The collection of reflections stems from years of helping busy people find their center and hear once again the quiet voice of God in their lives. The reflections will help you fine-tune your senses so that you can detect that seemingly undetectable whisper. They will be your compass as you tack and trim the sailboat of your storm-driven life.

Perhaps from time to time we can drop anchor and go ashore for some quiet R&R. We can go on a retreat or a vacation and spend some long, quiet days with God in prayer. But what of the majority of our days when our life does not allow us to slow down? Might we still keep attuned to God's voice, even in the midst of the clamor? That is what this book is for. We can take just a small moment in our crazy day, read a reflection, ponder the questions, and remember again that Christ, with one word, can still the storm and remind us that we have nothing to fear. Christ's ship (it's his and not ours!) is sturdy and unsinkable.

Please step out of your busy life for just a moment, take a breath, and enjoy *Discern: Listening for God's Whispers*.

MARK E. THIBODEAUX, SJ

Definitions

consolation: *a state where one feels spiritually uplifted, at peace, and in connection with God's presence. One feels a great desire to act out of faith, hope, and love.*

desolation: *a state where one feels spiritual emptiness, restlessness, or turmoil and feels distant from God's love. Rather than being "fired up" about faith, hope, and love, one might feel listless, resistant, uncomfortably anxious, or otherwise unmotivated.*

Tuning In

In any given situation, whether in an ordinary day or in a day of momentous decision, there are many voices in your head and heart proposing to you a variety of actions, reactions, or nonactions. The Ignatian method of discernment teaches you how to fine-tune your spiritual senses so that you can more readily detect and move toward the voice of the Good Shepherd, distinguishing that voice from all the others.

———————

To whom or what can you trace the voices in your head?

How fine-tuned would you say your spiritual senses are?

What can you do to further refine them?

Beyond Doing

Ignatius set out to teach people how to become a kind of person who, through a sort of learned intuition, could detect the sources of one's thoughts, emotions, and actions. Through that discernment of the sources, which he called the discernment of spirits, a person can determine God's will in any given situation. In other words, once a person can recognize the motivations moving her toward one particular choice or another, then the work of coming to a decision becomes easy: she simply chooses the option that comes from God. Ignatian discernment, then, isn't so much about what to do but about who to be. It's about becoming a person in tune with the movements that lead toward God. The doing will flow from the being.

Who do you know who has an intuition for detecting the sources of their thoughts, emotions, and actions and seems to be in tune with the movements that lead toward God?

What can you learn from this person?

Two Spirits

This recognition of "the difference between the two spirits that moved him" became the foundation of Ignatius's lifelong exploration of how a person discerns God's will. He came to believe that God, in infinite love and compassion for us, is at all times stirring our hearts with desires to do great deeds of life and love while another spirit leads us to lower dreams and moves us to act against the life-giving inspirations of God. Ignatius discovered that if a person could simply discern between these two spirits—the one pulling toward life and the other pulling away from life—then that person would know God's will.

To what extent are you aware of the two spirits moving within you?

What makes it difficult to distinguish between the two?

What helps you discern God's will?

Navigating the Distance

The experience of feeling distant from God is a strong sign of desolation. Worse yet is the lack of desire to be close to Christ. This, too, is a more common experience for believers than you might think. Even strong, faith-filled Christians go through times when they don't feel like praying, they don't want to go to church, and they resist spiritual renewal.

———————

Why is the lack of desire to be close to Christ even worse than the experience of feeling distant from God?

When was a time that you experienced this lack of desire and who or what helped restore that desire?

Sailing

The opposite of life, then, is not death but tepidity, tedious-ness, boredom, blandness, indifference, lethargy. None of these feelings is from the true spirit. In the spiritual life, St. Ignatius found this state far more distressing than the state of being at odds with God or agitated by spiritual disruptions. From my brother who sails I've learned that I can use any wind, from any direction, to get my sailboat back home. But if there is no wind at all, there is little that can be done.

———————

What can cause us to feel that there is no wind in our sails?

How do you, or how can you, help others get their sailboats back home?

The Truth about Fear

St. Ignatius says that for a person sincerely trying to find God's will, fear is not a tool of the true spirit. When fear is in our hearts, chances are, we are not focused on what God is saying to us. Later on, I will define consolation as letting God dream in me. If that is the case, then desolation is allowing the false spirit to nightmare in me. I am in desolation when I become preoccupied by false futures of impending doom. I become convinced that, just around the corner, things will go badly for me. Rather than remain in the present, I dwell on frightening possibilities that will never happen.

What fears does the false spirit sometimes nightmare within you?

What practices might better enable God to dream in you?

My God, My God

Part of the experience of desolation is the sense that God is distant from me. I can't feel a strong sense of God's presence. I feel spiritually abandoned and alone. I say the "sense" of God's absence or the "feeling" of being abandoned by God because faith assures me that God never abandons me. If God did so, I would cease to exist. God is always near, always watching and loving me—always acting for the good in my life. But I don't always feel that divine love. I can't always sense God's presence in my heart.

Describe a time when you felt that God was distant from you—a time when you couldn't sense his presence in your heart.

What experience or situation caused you to slip into this time of desolation?

What are the some of the prompts, strategies, or situations that help you experience a stronger sense of God's presence?

Lost

I am truly in the depths of desolation not simply when I experience dryness in prayer but also when I have lost the sense of hope and faith that this will ever change. In desolation, I am drawn to question not just this moment but my entire relationship with God. I will begin to wonder if my whole experience of God is just a sham, something I made up in my head. I will question the existence of God, or at least the existence of my friendship with God.

Have you experienced a time when you questioned your entire relationship with God?

Who or what helped you emerge from this experience of desolation?

Discerning the False Spirit's Influence

Inner disturbance or restlessness—what Ignatius called disquiet —may well be the most revealing characteristic of the false spirit because it is the disquietude about the other characteristics that reveals its source. Ignatius does not worry so much about "many disturbances and temptations" but rather about "disquiet from various agitations and temptations." There will always be agitations, negative feelings, temptations, and upsetting thoughts. What the discerner needs to pay attention to is the extent to which these negative movements within him disturb his peace of mind.

How can we prevent agitations, negative feelings, temptations, and upsetting thoughts from giving rise to a pervasive disquiet (inner disturbance and restlessness)?

What are the instigators that prove most disruptive to your peace of mind?

You Are What You Eat
(or, Feeding the Spirit)

A Native American legend tells of an elder explaining to his grandson that there are two wolves within him struggling for control of his actions. One wolf is the true spirit, and the other is the false spirit. The young grandson asks, "And which will win, Grandfather?" The old man answers, "The one I feed." This is precisely the point. I do not have a choice about having the two wolves within me. This side of heaven, I must deal with inner negativity. But I do have some choice in my attitude toward that negativity.

———

What does it mean to feed the spirits within us?

In what ways do you find yourself feeding the false spirit?

The true spirit?

Steering toward Peace and Quiet

"Agitations" will come and go in life. I can't stop them from coming. And often, when I make great efforts to kick them off the bus, they simply become more obstinate. Because I focus all my attention on them, they have now moved into the driver's seat. But if I allow the good spirit of Peace and Quiet to drive the bus, it isn't so distressing that Anger is a fellow passenger.

———

What agitations do you find driving your bus from time to time?

What can you do to move Peace and Quiet into the driver's seat?

Perspective

Unsettling confusion is indeed a common telltale sign of desolation. A person in this state is missing the forest for the trees. He loses his perspective of the ultimate goal of life, which is defined by St. Ignatius as "praise, reverence, and service of God our Lord." The confusion of desolation causes a person to get bogged down in the details of the journey while forgetting the ultimate destination. It's a failure to "keep your eyes on the prize." Otherwise, the state of not knowing would not be unsettling and therefore not desolating.

_____

What causes confusion or a loss of perspective in your life?

Who helps you regain perspective?

How do they accomplish this?

Bold Choices

Desolation can use even rational fears to stop me from acting boldly toward the good I'm called to do. In the Gospel Nativity stories, Joseph's fears of taking Mary for his wife were well founded. It's easy to imagine the trouble he would have to endure for marrying a pregnant girl in first-century Palestine. Joseph had good reason to fear. But even rational fear shouldn't be the driver of the bus. God sometimes calls me to do things that are genuinely frightening, and in those situations it's natural to be afraid. But I can choose not to feed and be fed by that fear. Rather, I can choose to act boldly, trusting in the promise that God will take care of those who follow his will.

When was a time that God called you to do something genuinely frightening?

How did you deal with the fear that came with this experience?

Beware the Enemy's Tricks

Ignatius warns against the false spirit's trick of getting me to keep things secret from my mentors and companions. Common sense requires that I not tell everyone everything all the time. However, if my companions and mentors are well chosen and are trustworthy, there is virtually no reason to keep any part of my inner life secret from them. If I find myself doing so, chances are, the false spirit is afoot. When I am in desolation, I cannot trust my own judgment; I will need the objectivity and sensibility of the wise and loving people around me. Otherwise, I will be lost in my own private fog and will not even be aware of the fog's existence. The spirit of desolation will attempt to leave me in this fog by keeping me from those who are standing outside it.

———————

What might you be keeping secret?

With whom do you share your secrets, and how does this person bring objectivity and sensibility to your life?

For whom do you perform a similar role?

Temptations in Disguise

False consolation is the experience of being drawn to feelings, thoughts, and motivations that look good and holy at first but that ultimately lead to actions to which God is not calling that person, or not calling that person to at that time. Once a Christian has begun to take her faith seriously—to pray, to attend church, to seek spiritual advice, and so on—she is not so tempted by blatant sin. Generally speaking, she is not as attracted by unloving acts, self-destructive behaviors, sexual promiscuity, and so on. For such a person, temptations may begin to come in the form of attractions to holy distractions that would keep her from her particular callings from God.

———————

What are examples of holy distractions?

How can something seemingly holy prevent us from hearing God's call?

In what ways do we use holy distractions as a defense mechanism to shield us from facing deeper issues and unresolved questions?

The Divine Presence

One of the strongest signs of consolation is the strong, deep, and lasting sense of God's presence. It's not enough simply to believe that God exists and that God is good. Deep in the soul, we have experienced God's presence and God's personal love for us. This is an intimacy in which God seems to be gazing at us directly and specifically. "By name I have called you," says God through the prophet Isaiah.

Have you ever had an experience of this strong, deep, lasting sense of God's presence?

Describe the experience and what precipitated it.

What fosters intimacy with God?

Primal Harmony

This divine love communicated between God's presence in me and God's presence in creation leads me to a transcendent synchronicity with creation. The rhythm of the universe pulses in sync with the primal pulse of my heart. I sense the pulse of God in all of it: first in my heart, then in birdsong, silent leaf, crying baby, and yes, even in idling car engine and droning refrigerator. It's all God's pulse—everywhere and in everything. In all these ordinary and mundane ways, says St. Ignatius, the good spirit's action is "delicate, gentle, delightful. It may be compared to a drop of water penetrating a sponge."

What helps you feel a transcendent synchronicity with God's creation? Explore your answer.

In what aspects of nature do you most sense the pulse of God?

Divine Calm

The peace of consolation is not peace "as the world gives" (John 14:27), which is merely the state of no conflict. Rather, the peace of consolation is the state of being at peace specifically about the various agitations and temptations of my life. This peace isn't a peace without problems, agitations, and so on. It isn't even peace despite problems. It is a divine peace about those difficult, unresolved issues of my life. I know that I have problems. I'm fully aware of the unpleasant and unredeemed aspects of my life. I may on the surface feel terribly upset, angry, or sad about them. But I have a sense deeper down that God is working through even these difficult parts of my life.

Who is someone you know that seems, more often than not, to possess the peace of consolation?

What can you learn from this person about experiencing the true peace of consolation? Describe.

Courage in Consolation

Looking at this peace and tranquility from another angle, we could call this characteristic of consolation courage as opposed to the paralyzing fear of desolation. Just as Christ's peace works through the agitations rather than despite them, so, too, does this courage work in the midst of fear but without eliminating it. The courage of consolation is an assured confidence that God will provide for those who are doing God's work. This is the peace, tranquility, and courage of consolation. It is an assurance and confidence in God in the midst of trials, limitations, past failures, and future dangers.

———————

When was a time that you had the courage or empowerment imparted by peace to move forward in the face of fear? Describe.

Who or what helps you have an assured confidence that God will provide?

Trust in God's Timing

Just as confusion could be called a subcategory of the disquiet of desolation, so could true perspective be a subcategory of peace and tranquility. A person experiencing consolation is well aware that she does not have all the answers. During early stages of discernment, she may not have any answers at all. But a consoled person does not sweat the problem, because she understands that this is a normal part of human experience and a healthy, perhaps even necessary, stage in good discernment. She is confused about the situation, but she keeps it in perspective. She remembers that she doesn't have to have the answers, because the One who is all-knowing is also all-powerful and all-good. She trusts that God will enlighten her mind when the time is right.

When was a time that you helped someone regain perspective?

Who helps you maintain or regain perspective?

Liberation through Transparency

We have already seen how the false spirit works through secrecy. The opposite can be said of the true spirit. "God is light and in him there is no darkness at all," says the first letter of John (1 John 1:5). There is no greater feeling than to bring some dark, private thought into the light. Sharing with a trusted loved one that which has been "kept in the dark" is a liberating experience.

———

When was a time that you felt liberated by sharing with someone else something you had been keeping to yourself?

What is something you are keeping in the dark that you desire to be liberated from? Ponder your response.

The Importance of Self-Reflection

Often, in the ordinary moments of my day, I act in a way that is inconsistent with my true self. I say something inappropriate; I ignore someone who is trying to reach out to me; I overreact; I gossip; I avoid important work; I yell at the cat. If I stopped and reflected on it a moment, I'd probably say to myself, "Wait a minute. This is not me. What is going on here?" If I scratch beneath the surface, I may discover some desolation lurking beneath. It could be psychological, emotional, or spiritual desolation, or more likely some combination of those. Simply naming the desolating factors beneath my exterior attitudes and actions can go a long way toward moving out of the desolation. If it does not disappear altogether at the moment I name it, then at least I can keep a leash on it.

What does it mean to keep a leash on desolating factors beneath our exterior attitudes and actions?

What inconsistent thoughts and actions of your own do you most feel the need and desire to leash? Ponder your response.

Avoid Rash Decisions

Whether desolation has been named or not, it generally makes a good, prayerful Christian very uncomfortable. Often the person will do something—anything—to get out of this discomfort. She may incorrectly conclude that some previous decision was wrong and so attempt to reverse that decision. Or she may think that she must do something different in order to get out of the funk. The problem is that a person loses objectivity when in desolation. Agitation, fear, and confusion lead the person to focus on changes that are at best unnecessary and at worst disastrous.

———

Describe a time when you came to, or narrowly avoided, a hasty decision while trying to reverse or extricate yourself from desolation. Who or what enabled you to regain objectivity?

The Power of Naming

Sadness, fear, boredom, or confusion begins to wear on the desolate person, and she begins to reason poorly. Conclusions she never would come to during a state of consolation suddenly appear to be the best—perhaps even the only—option. If in those desolate moments of my life I can succeed in the first directive, to name it as desolation, then my next conclusion should be to draw no more conclusions without careful consideration and counsel from those who have an objective point of view.

_____

When was a time that you witnessed someone lapse into a period of poor reasoning due to a loss of objectivity?

How have you helped counsel someone experiencing this?

Who has counseled you?

Support Networks

A popular series of cell-phone commercials boasted the strength of network coverage by showing a huge crowd of people following close behind the customer as he walked down the street speaking on his cell phone. That's a good metaphor for the kind of support I'm going to need if I am to live according to God's will. As I make my way through the spiritual life, it is absolutely crucial that I have a strong support network following close behind me, cheering me on, booing the false spirit, whispering tips in my ear, and passing me Gatorade. I will need good mentors, good companions, and a strong link to the church.

Who is in your network of support?

Describe times when people in your network have cheered you on, booed the false spirit, whispered helpful advice in your ear, or passed you the Gatorade.

Cultivate Supportive Relationships

We need to draw a distinction between a friend and a companion. Let us say that a friend is someone who enjoys my company and whose company I enjoy. I have a good time when he's around. I find myself laughing more, relaxing more. I like his sense of humor and his quirky mannerisms. It is a pleasure to be with him. But let's say a companion is all this and more. Let's say a companion is someone who deeply desires for me to be my best. A companion is someone who calls forth from me my best self and does so without being bossy, parental, or preachy.

Looking back on your life up to this point, who are the people that have served as companions?

Describe a time when one such companion called forth from you your best self without being bossy, parental, or preachy.

Church as Refuge

The church is the spiritual refuge for battle-weary souls. I attend church to pray with people who have the same great desires and insipid temptations as I. Together as one family, we lift our prayers to the Father, and we beg the Son to come close—to teach us, to heal us, to redeem us, and to befriend us. When I feel lost, confused, and frightened, the ritual of the church nourishes and strengthens me in a place too deep for words. Ritual allows my body to act out what my soul is longing to articulate. When I am spiritually starving, the Body and Blood are the rations that keep me alive another day. When I am drowning, I hold tight to the lifeline of the rosary. Without the food and without the light I wither. When I am blind and deaf, it is the smell of incense that raises my plea to the heavens.

_____

How does the Church offer you spiritual refuge?

What spiritual practices does the Church offer that bring healing to your battle-weary soul? Ponder how they might have helped you in your spiritual development.

Reach Out

When I am in desolation, the self-destructive movement within me will tend to sustain itself by convincing me that I should keep these thoughts, emotions, and actions to myself. Otherwise, a wise mentor or companion will quickly see the falsity in the movement and will help me rid myself of its devastating effects. The supports of my mentors, companions, and the church are my metaphorical fire extinguishers; when things flare up, I'll need to break the glass and put them to work!

———

When was a time that you eventually needed to break the glass and call on a mentor, companion, or church member to help you put out a fire in your life?

What prevents us from breaking the glass and asking for help?

Reflect on Moral Choices

Most of the time, desolation will come for reasons other than sin. There are times, however, when desolation is the natural consequence of my own attitudes, actions, or omissions. When I find myself in desolation, I should examine my conscience to explore whether I might have made a poor moral choice somewhere along the way. The fallout of sinful attitudes and actions will reverberate through every aspect of my life, including my prayer life. A more careful reading of Ignatius suggests that sinful inactions, what the church calls sins of omission, may be an even more common cause. He suggests that desolation might have come because "we are tepid, slothful, or negligent." Taking his advice, the person in desolation will want to look especially to those particular sins.

In what ways do sinful attitudes and actions reverberate through every aspect of our lives?

Why does Ignatius suggest that sins of omission may be a more common cause of desolation than sinful actions?

Renewal

Sometimes, the problem is not that I am doing something wrong in my prayer but simply that my prayer has gotten a little stale, and a change would be refreshing. Just because praying early in the morning has always worked for me in the past, I should not presume that it is the best time slot for me in the present. If meditation and contemplation are the center of my prayer life, perhaps I should grab my rosary and go for a walk for the next few days. I must remember that God is the one who does the heavy lifting in prayer and that God greatly desires for our relationship to deepen. Therefore, any attempt to reach for God will in fact reach God, even if I don't always sense God's presence.

In what ways have you attempted to make sure your prayer life has not grown stale?

What does it mean that, in prayer, God is the one who does the heavy lifting?

Addressing Desolation Holistically

Good Christians often make the mistake of thinking that there is something wrong with their moral lives when, in reality, the cause of the problem is psychological. If it is a fairly serious psychological problem, it would be impossible to find the solutions to the problem through prayer alone. It would be like consulting the Bible to learn how to make chicken gumbo. God has gifted the world with medical technology and with advances in psychotherapy. God wants us to receive these gifts and to utilize them as we proceed through life and continue to grow spiritually.

Why is prayer alone not enough when psychological problems are the cause of desolation?

How can prayer and psychology work together to help one grow spiritually?

The Danger of False Holiness

If I am currently in a state of desolation, then I am especially vulnerable to deception by the false angel of light. Any time the psyche is uncomfortable with its current state, it will work to flee the discomfort. For the devout Christian, escape from the pain will often be in the form of some "holy" action that is in fact not an appropriate response to the situation.

———

Describe a time when you observed someone who was in desolation fall victim to deception in hopes of fleeing discomfort.

How can "holy" actions stand in the way of a truly appropriate response?

Committing to Prayer

Many people in desolation either stop praying altogether or begin to skim a little off the top. If my daily practice is to pray for thirty minutes, for example, I may find myself leaving prayer after twenty or twenty-five minutes. It's not hard to imagine the following week slipping further down the slope to ten or fifteen minutes, and so on. During desolation, I may need to make a firm commitment to prayer. As recommended by Ignatius, I might want to make a symbolic gesture of resistance to the desolation by adding a few minutes to the end of it. If I find myself constantly looking at my watch during prayer, I might set the alarm for the designated time and put the watch out of reach.

_____

What does it mean to make a symbolic gesture of resistance to desolation?

What is an example from your own life of when you made a symbolic gesture to firm up your commitment to prayer?

Wait

Desolation is normally not the time for bold moves. Instead, if possible, I sit quietly and patiently, actively waiting for God to make the next move, and believing that he will. My own novice *master* once said, "If you're traveling on a horse through the desert and a sandstorm kicks up, get off your horse, lie face down on the ground, and wait it out." If at all possible, I lie low for a while and try to enjoy this low-profile life.

Do you find it challenging to sit quietly, patiently, waiting for God to make the next move?

What does it mean to lay low and keep a low profile during times of desolation?

Growth through Suffering

Desolation is not a wasted period. It's an opportunity to receive the more difficult graces that can come only through a bit of suffering. Remember that, while God never brings desolation, God does allow it and would never do so unless we could grow from the experience. It was through the experience of crying out to God that Job encountered God in a transcendent way. And through this experience of desolation and redemption, Job became far more blessed (wiser, holier, more successful) than before the desolation. Like Job, I can look back at the darkest times of my life and see that it was in those times that I grew the most.

When was a time that you received the more difficult graces and grew from an experience of suffering or desolation?

Is there a period in your life that you consider as having been wasted because of desolation?

Do you need to seek grace so that you can reframe this period of time not as having been wasted but rather as an experience of growth?

Spiritual Wellness

Asking what to do when in consolation is like going to my doctor to ask if there is anything I should do about all this good health I've been having lately. I presume the doctor would say, "Go live!" And so it is with consolation. My chief task is to go live! To go do something beautiful with my life. But healthy people do, in fact, go to see their doctors. They go for a checkup, which involves various tests to determine if there are unseen problems and also to prevent potential problems from ever existing. And so, aside from my chief task of living out my First Principle and Foundation, I should do regular checkups when in consolation to discern underlying spiritual problems or to prevent potential problems from occurring.

In what ways is asking what to do during consolation like going to the doctor to find out if there's anything you should do about all the good health you've been having?

Why is consolation an ideal time to do regular checkups on your spiritual wellness?

Facing Fear and Pain

If consolation is the ideal time to work on desolations, then why are we so hesitant to do so? Often we hesitate to look at the painful parts of life because we're using the defense mechanism of avoidance. The psyche is programmed to fear psychological pain. We engage in avoidance in order to pretend that the problems do not exist. But we have already seen that fear is not a preferred tool of the true spirit. It's not wise to act out of fear—even if the action is to avoid doing something that would help. And to pretend that desolation won't come again is to remain naive and unprepared.

What is your response to the question that begins this paragraph?

What problem(s) or psychological pain might you be avoiding at this point in your life? How might this avoidance be affecting your day-to-day?

Learning from Spiritual Lows

Once I have "detected and recognized by the trail of evil" the false spirit and have ascended out of the pit of desolation, Ignatius instructs me to go back and follow the course of thoughts that led me into the desolation. What was the perceivable beginning of my desolation? What was my state of being just before that? What were my life circumstances around that time? Were there any exterior shifts that could have caused interior disquietude? Did anything upset me at that time? Did anything excite me or make me happy? Were there any important moments in my significant relationships?

Why does Ignatius instruct us to revisit our desolation when we are in consolation? Isn't this like reopening a wound?

Was there a time when you were able to pinpoint the precise, perceivable beginning of an experience of desolation? How did you respond?

Addressing Vulnerabilities

While I must attend to the immediate consequences of my vulnerabilities during desolation, I should explore the underlying causes of them while in consolation. While in desolation, I do what I need to quickly "plug the hole" so that more trouble doesn't come. While in consolation, I work on the ground zero of my vulnerabilities, and I work on more lasting solutions.

_____

How does one work on the ground zero of one's vulnerabilities, as well as on lasting solutions?

Describe a time when you or someone you know needed to plug the hole during desolation but was later able to explore the underlying causes during consolation.

Recognizing Triggers

Often, desolation comes through the portal of one of my points of vulnerability. Desolation will push my buttons. If I am prone to rage, desolation will provide things for me to get angry about. If I have low self-esteem, it will have me fixate on and exaggerate some criticism I've received recently. If I'm lazy, the TV remote will beckon as I set out to pray. The more I'm aware of my own weaknesses, the more I'll be able to recognize when the false spirit is going after them. During consolation, when I am clearheaded, Ignatius encourages me to reflect about this.

What do you consider to be your own points of vulnerability?

What pushes your buttons?

How can it help to reflect on these realities of life?

HALT

Members of Alcoholics Anonymous learn that, even more basic than these defense mechanisms, simple human urgings sometimes compel us to do stupid things. When a recovering alcoholic is tempted to drink, she is taught to "HALT" and ask herself if some basic human need is not being met: Am I hungry, angry, lonely, or tired? It's important to remember that often, without my knowing it, my unconscious is reacting to some threat, hurt, or need. The more I bring these problems into the level of consciousness in my prayer, the less likely will desolation use them to get the best of me.

What are examples of simple human urgings that can compel us to do stupid things?

What is something you did in the past that you now feel stupid for?

How have you learned to not let such situations get the best of you?

Prudence

Sometimes the intoxicating consolation that immediately follows a profound experience—an intense religious retreat, a conversion or reconversion, a near-death or other mystical experience—will move a person to do something spiritually bold but not very prudent. For example, after a life-changing religious retreat, a young person might, without thorough discernment, attempt to join a monastery or become a lay missionary in Africa. While consolation is a good time to discern and act boldly, we should never do so without considering it "very carefully." All our actions, even those springing from consolation, should be "carefully examined."

———————

What is the most spiritually bold thing you've ever done?

In retrospect, was it prudent?

Why or why not?

Finding God in Desolation

When in desolation, I am often incapable of sensing God's presence in my life. During those difficult periods, I must simply choose to believe that God is present, even though I have no evidence. During consolation, then, it is important to look back on those dark moments in order to recognize the hand of God in them. One of the chief characteristics of consolation is the ease with which a person can "find God in all things," to use an Ignatian phrase. Looking backward to see how God was with me, guiding me, loving me all along, will increase the joy of consolation and help me act in faith—confidence in God's presence—the next time I am in desolation.

Describe an experience of desolation in which, upon looking back, you now recognize the hand of God.

What are some events in your life that you need to recall in search of the hand of God?

The Need for Guidance

When we feel strong, healthy, and happy, we are tempted to discontinue our visits with directors and mentors. We think that because we're fine, we no longer need those visits. But Ignatius would beg to differ. If we're really going to work on reviewing the past desolation, on shoring up vulnerabilities, on looking out for false consolation, and on seeking God in the painful parts of the past, we will need the objectivity that only someone on the outside of the experience can provide. There are simply too many temptations for denial and avoidance as we work on these touchy areas of life.

Why is it wise to have someone on the outside to talk to during good times and bad?

Who brings objectivity to your perspective? How does this person affect your life?

Life's Multiple Callings

What are my vocations in life—what am I called to do with my life? Note that the word vocations is plural here; we are searching for ways to discern our big vocations such as marriage, single life, or religious life, but we are also interested in our smaller vocations: Where am I called to live? Who am I called to befriend? What work am I called to do and where? And we are even interested in how we might discern the smaller stuff that comes up in the course of a day: Should I confront the boss about this? Should I work on this little project or that one? Should I steer our group into moving in this direction or that one? Should I call in sick today or buck up and go to work?

Make a list of your vocations—the things you are called to do with your life—whether big or small.

Why is it important to discern our small vocations, as well as our big vocations?

The Grace of Gratitude

There's much diversity among the saints, mystics, and other spiritual heroes. They express a variety of personalities, gifts, and callings. But one characteristic that seems to permeate the prayers of them all is gratitude. This is no less true of St. Ignatius of Loyola. His classic Spiritual Exercises, which is designed to guide a person through a thirty-day retreat, is chock-full of gratitude. Indeed, gratitude is the underlying grace Ignatius seeks for the repentant retreatant. He wishes for the retreatant to take a long sober look at her sinfulness precisely because it was in reflecting on Ignatius's own sinful past that he became smitten with the love and mercy of God.

What are you most grateful for at this moment in your life?

How does looking at our sinfulness lead us to gratitude?

Describe an example from your own experience.

Will and Desire

Every decision maker must begin discernment by asking the big questions—must set down for herself the foundation and purpose of all her actions. Ignatius was convinced that if the soul were truly in touch with its deepest desires, it would find itself wanting nothing more than to praise, reverence, and serve God—wanting nothing more than to glorify God with one's life. It is the deepest desire of all and is the ultimate source of all other desires. Once a person names that greatest desire of all, she then finds herself ready to give up whatever does not lead to the glory of God and ready to take on whatever will lead to the greater glory of God.

As you reflect on your greatest desires, what comes to mind?

In what ways are these desires connected with praising, reverencing, and serving God?

Passionate Indifference

Ignatian indifference is quite different from what is normally referred to as indifference—that is, the negative attitude of not caring about something. On the contrary, Ignatian indifference is filled with passion—passion for the will of God and the good of all. If I am indifferent in this Ignatian sense, then I care so much about serving God in a quite definite way that I am willing and ready to take on anything—or give up anything—for the cause. Ignatian indifference does not ignore desires but rather taps into our deepest desire—our desire to praise, reverence, and serve God.

How can indifference be filled with passion?

What does it mean to you to practice indifference as Ignatius defines it? Ponder your response.

Finding Stillness

The modern world, for all its marvels, is simply too noisy for our own good. We cannot think straight with the cacophony of competing values presented by advertisements, the media, politicians, and the people around us. In order to hear the sound of God's voice, we must turn down the sound of the world. We must come to a place of stillness within by separating ourselves from the noise outside. Even for an experienced discerner, the movements of the spirits are simply too subtle to detect without quieting down for a little while each day.

———

When and where can you turn down the sound of the world in order to be in touch with the subtle movements of the spirits?

What can you do on a regular basis to turn down the volume of your noisy world?

The Intimacy of Prayer

Having a prayer life involves more than simply praying every day. It is a core experience of my day-to-day life. Prayer does not necessarily take up a lot of my time, but it does take up a lot of my interior space, in terms of its impact on the whole of my life. I understand prayer as crucial to my well-being. When a companion sincerely asks "How are you?" the state of my prayer life will be an important part of my answer. It is almost as if my prayer life were a person with whom I am in a loving relationship: I care for it, nurture it, and give my whole heart to it. My prayer life, in turn, nurtures me, grounds me, and gives me direction.

———

How does prayer take up not just time but also interior space?

If your prayer life were a person with whom you are in a loving relationship, how healthy would you say that relationship is? Ponder your response in your heart.

Tension and Choices

Important decisions are hard to make and involve an inner tension that begs to be resolved. I am tempted, then, to do one of two things with my decision. I may be tempted to jump too fast—to resolve the tension by making a quick (and rash) act and be done with it. Or I may be tempted not to jump at all—to pretend to be working on the decision, all the while hoping that it resolves itself. It may indeed resolve itself, but not necessarily in the way God wills.

––––––––––

What kind(s) of inner tension are you carrying with you now?

Do you lean toward jumping too fast to resolve tension, or not dealing with it at all in the hopes that it will be resolved without intervention?

Finding God in Our Desires

Many spiritual writers of Ignatius's day spoke of desires as obstacles to God's will. A person was supposed to suppress his desires—to eliminate them whenever possible. But Ignatius held the radical notion that God dwells within our desires. Not only are desires not evil, but they are also one of God's primary instruments of communicating to us. God inflames the heart with holy desires and with attractions toward a life of greater divine praise and service. Unlike many of his religious contemporaries of the sixteenth century, Ignatius did not seek to quash desires but to tap into the deepest desires of the heart, trusting that it is God who has placed them there.

Does it surprise you that Ignatius advocated we not repress *our desires but rather* tap into *them? Explore your answer.*

How does God use our desire as one of his primary instruments for communicating with us?

Understanding Sin through Ignatian Wisdom

Desires, of course, do play a role in our sinful choices. But Ignatius would define sin as disordered desire. The problem is not that we have desires but that they are disordered—that is, out of balance or too heavily influencing our decisions. That is why we need to begin this entire process by tapping into the greatest, most universal desires of all: to praise, reverence, and serve God. We fall into sin when we are ignorant of the true, God-given desires beneath the apparent desires. We sin, not because we are in touch with our desires, but precisely because we are not in touch with them! This is one of Ignatius's most radical and most profound insights.

What does Ignatius mean when he describes sin as "disordered desires"?

How can being deeply in touch with our desires lead us away from sin instead of into sin?

Recognizing Peace in Spiritual Decisions

Ignatius says that when a well-intentioned, prayerful person is in consolation, God's will comes "sweetly, lightly, gently, as a drop of water that enters a sponge." These descriptors are among the most important telltale signs of God's will in the particular option I am considering. When I ponder my praydreams, which of the options left me feeling this way? Which leave me with a sense of deep-down peace? Note that I am searching for the deep-down peace, as opposed to simply feeling comfortable with the option.

Describe experiences you have had of feeling profound peace immediately after a period of discernment.

Did God's will come to you sweetly, lightly, gently? Explore your answer.

When the Heart Knows the Way

Often, after many hours of prayerful deliberation, there will be a moment when a person just knows. It will feel not as though I am making a decision, but rather as though I am acknowledging a decision that my heart has already made. I'll recognize this auspicious moment by the way one option over the others leads to praydreams that are maybe not as idealistic or beautiful as when I first began to dream them but are somehow more realistic and right. These dreams will fit like a glove. All the other options—though perhaps more beautiful, more comfortable, or safer—will drift farther from my soul's watchful eye and will begin to fade into the horizon.

What does it mean that sometimes, after prayer, a person just knows?

When was a time that a dream or choice fit like a glove for you? Ponder your response.

Presenting Our Decisions to God

Ignatius says that after the decision has been made, I am to "offer" God our Lord the decision so that God "may . . . accept and confirm it if it is for His greater service . . ." (emphases mine). The implications of these few words are strong: After the decision, I offer it to God, who may (or may not) confirm it. If it is not conducive to God's greater (Magis) service, then God presumably will not confirm the offering of the tentative decision. Clearly, then, though I have made a thorough and well-reflected decision, I am not quite finished with Ignatian discernment. Ignatius knows what a tricky process discernment can be, and he provides one last opportunity for God to throw me off my horse if I'm not quite going in the right direction.

How do we offer a decision to God?

Why is this a key step in the process of discernment?

How does God confirm a decision or choice we have made?

God's Guidance

Another way to seek confirmation of consolation is to notice how easily or how laboriously the doors open as I move toward the option I've tentatively chosen. This is what Ignatius meant by tranquility. Usually, if it is of God, I won't have to force my way in—I won't have to shove the doors open. God typically smooths the path and removes the obstacles when I am stepping in the right direction. Ignatius says that confirmation will be "easing and taking away all obstacles, so that the person may go forward in doing good."

Who helped open "doors for you as a sign" of God's confirmation of a choice you made?

When have you helped open doors for someone else who needed confirmation of a choice they made? Reflect on your response.

Spiritual Unease

Ignatius describes the phenomenon this way: for the person who is gradually maturing in relationship with God, God's will comes as water falling on a sponge: time and circumstance seem to soak it up. If my decision is not of God's will, the steps I take in acting out this decision will be like the ocean crashing against a craggy shore: there is no absorption, no easy marriage between the new decision and my present life. There is instead conflict, incongruity, and unease.

―――――

Describe a time when you continued to feel conflict, incongruity, and unease after a decision.

What was God trying to tell you through this experience, and what did you eventually end up doing?

Patience in Discernment

After a long and thorough discernment process, receiving no confirmation may be discouraging and frustrating. Where have I gone wrong? Was all that discernment misguided? Why won't God just tell me what he wants? This could be a painful moment in my discernment process. If it is, then I need to acknowledge my frustration and take it to prayer. As best I can, I must be patient with the process, with myself, and with God.

———————

Do you consider yourself patient with the process of seeking God's confirmation of your discernment? Explore your answer.

Who or what helps you grow in your patience?

Community and Spiritual Choices

If you have identified yourself as a hesitant decision maker, then you need to be careful to guard against the temptation of perpetually seeking confirmation. I do not believe that God typically desires for a person to remain in this awkward in-between place for very long. If you are hesitant, you may need the help of your support network to push you toward a final decision. If, however, you are naturally hasty, this awkward in-between time will seem excruciating! You will want badly to move into the final decision and throw caution to the wind. Hasty decision makers will need the help of their support network to cool their jets and wait patiently for confirmation.

———————

Who has helped either slow you down or push you forward when you were facing a decision you needed to make?

How did they do this?

When and how have you done this for others?

The Pledge

If the decision is one of lasting import, then after a while, consider making a pledge or firm commitment to the choice you have made—provided there isn't already a vow built in, such as in the case of marriage or religious profession. This, too, is to prevent the false spirit any wiggle room to take back the ground you have gained. A religious pledge, commitment, or vow will keep you strong and stable on the days when you feel weak and tempted to turn back.

What are the benefits of making a pledge to a choice you've made?

What might such a pledge look like?

Embrace Uncertainty

God never promises certainty. Sometimes I'll have it, but often I won't. Often I'll simply have to make my choice, not knowing for sure that it is the better choice but trusting that God knows my heart and will bless me for the attempt to do his will, even if I accidently miss the mark.

Why is it unrealistic to expect certainty when making a choice?

When was a time that, after having made a choice, you moved forward even though you weren't certain it was the correct choice?

The Greater

In cases without serious moral implications (choosing to attend one university over another, for example), it may well be that there is more than one correct choice and that God is ready to bless my life regardless of my choice. St. Ignatius calls this situation "choosing between goods." In these cases, then, what I am seeking is not the correct choice over a series of incorrect ones but rather the choice that is the Magis (the greater). That is, I am seeking the choice that will better aid me in achieving the purpose for which I am created (my principle and foundation). The fact that there may be more than one correct choice should relieve me on the days when I am intimidated by the decision I'm called to make.

Describe an experience when you were choosing between goods.

What does it mean to describe such a choice as "selecting the one that is the Magis"?

Living God's Gifts

What is crucial is my motivation for choosing. And what is crucial is that I offer to God this choice and all the other choices of my life. God has given me all these good gifts: family, education, opportunity, a passionate heart, and so on. My great desire is to use these gifts to bring about God's greater praise, reverence, and service—to give back to God the gifts that God has given me.

What are the greatest gifts God has given you?

How can you use these gifts to bring about God's greater praise, reverence, and service to others?

Spiritual Moods

When we are in a mood of listening to the evil spirit—when we are "driving under the influence" of the evil spirit—Ignatius says that we're in desolation. Today, when we say, "I'm in a bad space right now," we often mean that the evil spirit has gotten hold of us and we're struggling not to follow it. When we are in a mood of listening to the good spirit—Ignatius calls this consolation—we say, "I'm in a good space."

What does it mean to describe yourself as being "in a bad space right now"?

Describe what this feels like.

Describe what it feels like to be in a good space.

The Challenge of Difficult Consolation

We have learned that St. Teresa of Calcutta had terrible interior struggles for decades. The experience is painfully laid out in the posthumously published memoir *Come Be My Light*. How could someone who was so in sync with God and who so obviously passionately pursued faith, hope, and love be considered to be in desolation all that time? It seems to me that as we traditionally think of consolation and desolation, Mother Teresa simply doesn't fit the categories. However, she could be the patron saint of those in difficult consolation. [In difficult consolation,] we might experience grief, psychological depression, righteous anger, and fear, yet still be in sync with God and have great desires for faith, hope, and love.

What is meant by the term "difficult consolation"?

How can we be in sync with God and yet still experience grief, depression, anger, and fear?

The Dangers of Forcing Spiritual Consolation

When we are in desolation, we want badly to move to consolation (duh!). The problem is that, rather than allowing God to take us there at God's own slow pace, we impatiently try to force our way there on our own. This leads to disaster because not allowing the Lord to lead us is, by definition, desolation. We will never get to the promised land of consolation by this path. Instead, we will find ourselves in a self-manufactured consolation, which of course is just another type of desolation. If you will, the arrow of our heart, aiming for consolation, ricochets off an impenetrable wall and lands us in false consolation.

_____

What is the problem with self-manufactured consolation?

What or who helps you not force a way through to consolation on your own?

Trust the Process

North Americans are a product-centered people. Talk and reflection are worthless to us if the concrete and visible result does not immediately follow. Because of this we are impatient with the seemingly amorphous stages of discernment. We want the step-by-step directions that will get us to our destination with no meanderings. But because we are talking about communication with God, most of the process of good discernment is organic and somewhat vague. We need to make our peace with that fact.

What does it mean that we tend to be product-centered, and how does this affect our approach to discernment?

Have you made peace with the fact that the process of good discernment is organic and somewhat vague?

Divine Affections

Sometimes it seems that God just wants to give us a Big Kiss. God is not trying to change the trajectory of our lives or reveal a divine secret. God just wants to give us a Big Kiss for no particular reason other than that God loves us irresistibly. I've had numerous such experiences—times when I felt that I was more joyful than I had a right to be, more hopeful than the moment called for, more at peace than this world could ever promise. From time to time, God seems to give me a random, inexplicable, uncalled-for Big Kiss.

_____

What does it mean that, sometimes, God just wants to give us a Big Kiss?

Describe a time when this happened to you.

What was your reaction?

Managing Spiritual Elation and Its Aftereffects

Anyone who works in youth retreat ministry knows about the dangers of the "retreat high." If a youth retreat goes well and the retreatants are deeply moved by the end of it, they often feel an extraordinary happiness that makes them a little giddy. Often, this will lead to imprudent and irrational behavior such as immediately breaking up with a girlfriend or boyfriend or vowing to pray daily for an unreasonable quantity of time. This phenomenon is so common that leaders sometimes warn retreatants about it near the end of the retreat. And while it is easier to observe in youth because of their inclinations toward high drama, the retreat-high experience is almost as prevalent in adults.

When was a time that you experienced a high after participating in a religious or spiritual event?

Describe how you felt.

Why does this experience sometimes lead to imprudent and irrational behavior, and how can this be avoided?

Trust during Desolation

Ignatius says that a person in desolation has the false spirit as her counselor. Therefore she will not be able to rely on her own instincts and judgment at that moment. Instead, she should hand over the car keys—so to speak—of her decisions to the people around her who have good judgment and who care for her: her spiritual advisers, her family, her healthy friends. She should also lean on the support services of her church, such as the sacraments, communal prayer experiences, and the wisdom and teaching of the church.

To whom do you hand over the metaphorical car keys when you find yourself in a bad space (desolation)?

Who entrusted you with their metaphorical car keys when they found themselves in a bad space?

What did you do to be helpful in their moment of need?

Articulation and Spiritual Trauma

A psychologist I know once defined the term trauma as "experience seeking articulation." She said that when a person has an experience she has no way of articulating for herself, it is traumatic for her. The same is true for desolation. It is a traumatic experience because the person has not yet found a way to articulate the experience. Once she has put into words what she is experiencing, she may still be in desolation, but it won't be nearly as traumatic. And sometimes, finding the proper articulation can quickly lead to a way out of the desolation.

Why is articulation so important for dealing with trauma?

How is desolation a traumatic experience?

Who or what helps you articulate your thoughts and feelings when you are in desolation?

Preventing Spiritual Contagion

A wise saying has been passed down from one Jesuit novice director to the next: "When a novice enters your office with a monkey on his back, do what *you* can to help him get it off of him. But make sure that monkey doesn't jump on your back." Desolation is contagious. I can catch it from my directee if I am not diligent about my own spiritual and psychological well-being. When working with someone in desolation, I need to do my own work to make sure that I'm leaving it behind me as I leave my office at the end of the day. I need my own pressure-release valves that allow me to process the experience and to let it go.

In what ways can desolation be contagious?

What are some pressure-release valves that allow you to process experiences of helping someone in desolation so that you can leave it at the office and not bring it home with you?

Guarding against
Spiritual Complacency

I have a Jesuit friend who frequently annoyed me by responding to some great report I was giving about my life by saying, "That's wonderful, Mark. Now, how might the false spirit use this experience?" I hated this question. I just wanted to bask in the warmth of the consoling feelings. But my older and wiser friend taught me that both spirits can use any situation to move me toward their agendas. My friend was moving me to "remain sober and alert." (See 1 Peter 5:8)

How can the false spirit use your experience of consolation to try to move you toward desolation?

How does one remain sober and alert to this possibility?

Storing Strength for Future Challenges

Ignatius famously instructs the one in consolation to "let him consider how he will conduct himself during the time of ensuing desolation, and store up a supply of strength as defense against that day." Is Ignatius being morbid here? No, he simply is being pragmatic. It is in a time of consolation, when the good spirit is guiding us, that we can work on the spiritual and psychological issues that keep us from coping with desolation well.

How do you seek to store up strength during periods of consolation in preparation for later periods of desolation?

Do you think it's paranoid to do this?

Why or why not?

The "Black Box" Approach to Spiritual Growth

How is it that we humans have come to the point of so few accidental commercial plane crashes? It's simple: over the decades, after each crash we have recovered the "black boxes" that have meticulously recorded every moment of the ill-fated flight, from the preparations, through the takeoff, to the moment of the crash. The experts carefully study every tiny bit of every recorded datum. From this experience, they can usually diagnose the problem and work on a preventative solution. We should do the same with desolation. Once we have recovered from our "crash," we should extract the "black boxes" of data about the experience in order to diagnose the contributing factors and work on preventative solutions.

What black boxes have you recovered from experiences of desolation in your life?

What have you learned from the data you've recovered?

How has this helped you develop preventative strategies?

Resilience against the False Spirit

The false spirit is not very creative or innovative. Time and again, it attacks us in the very same "places" in our souls and psyches. This is great news for us! If we discover and fortify those spots while we're in the empowering moments of consolation, then the false spirit will have a tougher time getting through that "weakest point" the next time.

What would you describe as the weak points that make you vulnerable to the actions of the false spirit?

What have you done, or what can you do, to fortify these weak spots?

Honoring Sacred Moments

A friend and I used to have a saying: when one of us was sharing a deep moment of consolation that seemed to be of this "without cause" nature and would then begin to overanalyze the experience, the other would say, "Don't scribble on the altar." That was code for "Hey, buddy, just enjoy the sacred moment—enjoy the Big Kiss." We see this happening to Peter at the Transfiguration (Luke 9:33) After the experience of consolation without previous cause, we, like Peter, know not what we are saying. When we try to "make three tents"—that is, build a shrine to our consolation—we tend to spoil the moment and we sound a little loopy. Better not to scribble on the altar but rather to hush and to relish the Big Kiss.

What does it mean to tell someone in consolation not to "scribble on the altar"?

How do we, like Peter, sometimes attempt to build a shrine to our consolation?

How do we avoid doing so?

Suscipe

Take, Lord, and receive all my liberty,
my memory, my understanding,
and my entire will,
All I have and call my own.
You have given all to me.
To you, Lord, I return it.
Everything is yours; do with it what you will.
Give me only your love and your grace,
that is enough for me.

—St. Ignatius of Loyola

My Reflections

_____

_____

_____

_____

_____

_____

_____

_____

_____

_____

_____

_____

_____

_____

_____

_____

_____

My Reflections

_____

_____

_____

_____

_____

_____

_____

_____

_____

_____

_____

_____

_____

_____

_____

_____

_____

My Reflections

_____

_____

_____

_____

_____

_____

_____

_____

_____

_____

_____

_____

_____

_____

_____

_____

My Reflections

_____
_____
_____
_____
_____
_____
_____
_____
_____
_____
_____
_____
_____
_____
_____
_____

My Reflections

_____

_____

_____

_____

_____

_____

_____

_____

_____

_____

_____

_____

_____

_____

_____

_____

My Reflections

My Reflections

_____

_____

_____

_____

_____

_____

_____

_____

_____

_____

_____

_____

_____

_____

_____

_____

_____